Origins of
CHINESE
FOOD CULTURE

Illustrated by Fu Chunjiang   Translated by Qiu Yao Hong

⚖ ASIAPAC • SINGAPORE

Publisher
ASIAPAC BOOKS PTE LTD
996 Bendemeer Road #06-09
Singapore 339944
Tel: (65) 6392 8455
Fax: (65) 6392 6455
Email: asiapacbooks@pacific.net.sg

Come visit us at our Internet home page
www.asiapacbooks.com

First published January 2003

© 2003 ASIAPAC BOOKS, SINGAPORE
ISBN 981-229-318-3

Cover illustrations by Fu Chunjiang
Cover design by Kelly Lim
Body text in 11pt Times New Roman
Printed in Singapore by Loi Printing

Publisher's Note

Chinese cuisine is renowned the world over for its rich palette of flavours and endless variety. Equally extraordinary is the ancient culture from which it springs, with its vast treasury of myths and legends about the long-ago people and events that shaped the traditions and skills we know today.

We at Asiapac Books are pleased to present this volume, *Origins of Chinese Food Culture*, as part of our series on Chinese culture. In this book, you will learn about the exacting requirements of Chinese cuisine, as well as the fine arts associated with it and dining etiquette. See how eating habits have changed through the ages, and marvel at some of the more unusual customs and beliefs.

Here also, you will also find many fascinating tales about the origins of various customs and uncover the strange and wonderful beginnings of some of the most ubiquitous foods that seem so familiar and ordinary today. We hope that this book will help enhance your enjoyment and appreciation of Chinese food culture.

We would like to thank Mr Fu Chunjiang for his lively illustrations, and Mr Qiu Yao Hong for his translation. Our appreciation also goes to the production team for their efforts in putting this book together.

Chinese Culture Series (comics)
Origins of Chinese Festivals
Origins of Chinese Cuisine
Origins of Chinese People and Customs
Origins of Chinese Music and Art
Origins of Chinese Folk Arts
Origins of Chinese Martial Arts
Origins of Tibetan Culture
Origins of Chinese Food Culture
Origins of Chinese Medicine

About the Illustrator

Fu Chunjiang 傅春江, born in 1974, is a native of Chongqing municipality in southeastern China's Sichuan province. He has been fond of drawing ever since childhood and graduated in Chinese language studies. Fu loves traditional Chinese culture and has tried his hand at drawing comics.

Since 1994 he has been drawing comics and his works include *The Story of Kites* and *The Faint-hearted Hero*. He has also participated in the production of *One Riddle for One Story*.

His works like *Golden Rules for Business Success, Origins of Chinese Festivals* and *The Chinese Code of Success: Maxims by Zhu Zi* published by Asiapac Books are widely acclaimed.

CHINESE CULTURE SERIES

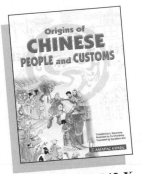

ISBN 981-229-242-X
160pp, B/W comics

ISBN 981-229-243-8
160pp, B/W comics

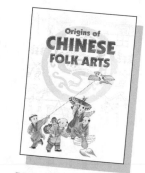

ISBN 981-229-264-0
160pp, B/W comics

ISBN 981-229-268-3
160pp, B/W comics

ISBN 981-229-317-5
160pp, B/W comics

ISBN 981-229-318-3
160pp, B/W comics

ISBN 981-3068-61-2
240pp, B/W comics

Contents

There is a Chinese saying, "Food is the first necessity of the people." Not only do Chinese love to eat, they love to cook too. Chinese cuisine is also well known worldwide, and Chinese restaurants can be found everywhere in the world.

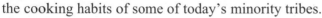

The History of Cooking

In primitive society, food was eaten raw, which often caused sickness. After the discovery of fire, people found that not only did the meat cooked with fire taste better, they didn't fall sick so often too.

In those days there weren't any cooking tools such as stoves and pans, so how did they cook? We can get some clues from the cooking habits of some of today's minority tribes.

The top part of the word *zhi* (roast) looks like a piece of meat, and the bottom part looks like fire. It means cooking meat over fire, which is the earliest form of cooking.

Bamboo Rice

Cut down a bamboo tube and make a hole at one end.

Add in rice and water.

Cork the hole and place the tube in fire.

Burn the tube until it turns yellow, and cut it open with a knife.

The rice is ready for serving.

The Origins of Cooking

Tong Yu was the third wife of Yellow Emperor. She took care of the basic needs of everyday life, such as food, shelter, and transportation.

Are you all right?

I'm fine. This happens all the time.

They always get stomachaches. Perhaps it has something to do with the diet.

I'll go with you on your next hunt.

The First Chef

The Chinese food and beverage industry has a tradition of praying to Peng Zu. It has been said that Peng Zu lived to almost 800 years old and had cooked for Di Yao, a legendary monarch in ancient China.

Some believe that the Yellow Emperor (Huang Di) was the first chef ever. The Yellow Emperor made a cauldron and taught his people to use the stove to steam millet into gruel.

There was also Sui Ren, who taught his people to start fires through friction. That was how Man learnt how to use fire to cook.

In the early days of the Shang Dynasty, a "God of Cookery" appeared. He was Yi Yin, prime minister to King Cheng Tang. Yi Yin once carried his cooking utensils and used cooking methods and flavourings to persuade King Cheng Tang to take up leadership of the state and successfully overthrow the corrupt Xia Dynasty.

Yi Yin Explains The World Through Cookery

Ancient Cooking Utensils

The three dynasties of Xia, Shang, and Zhou marked an important period in the history of Chinese cooking. It was during this period that the basic form of Chinese cuisine took shape. Developments in agriculture and animal husbandry also greatly expanded the food source. *The Book of Songs* was a collection of poems and songs that showed life during the Western Zhou Dynasty and the mid Spring and Autumn Period. The book mentioned over 130 types of plants, over 200 types of animals, as well as flavourings such as salt, soya sauce, honey, ginger, cinnamon, and chilli. The book also noted the "Eight Delicacies" of Chinese cuisine.

Culinary techniques also improved greatly during this period. Cooking utensils during the Xia Dynasty were mainly made of clay, while the Shang Dynasty was the period when bronze flourished. A huge bronze *ding* was even big enough to cook a calf. *Fu* was used for boiling soup, *li* for cooking porridge, and *zeng* for steaming rice. The diversity in cooking vessels showed that cooking had become a truly specialised skill.

What do the Eight Delicacies in Chinese refer to? The names on the list differ from period to period, and are divided into grades as well. The top grade includes monkey's lip, camel's hump, monkey's head, bear's paw, bird's nest, bird's gizzard, deer's tendon, and fish lip gum. The second grade includes shark's fin, tremella (a white fungus), masked civet, hilsa herring, fish maw, forest frog, dried sturgeon's lip, and calipash (meat at soft-shell turtle's shell skirt). The third grade includes sea cucumber, asparagus, *kou* mushroom (*Zhang Jiakou* dried mushroom), bamboo shoot, red-scale fish, dried scallop, oyster, and cuttlefish egg glands. The most common Eight Delicacies are dragon's liver, phoenix's marrow, leopard's foetus, carp's tail, roasted osprey meat, yellow weasel's lip, bear's paw, and crispy cicada.

Cooks and Dieticians

During the Xia Dynasty, the title 'cook' already existed for the person in charge of cooking. During the Zhou Dynasty, the royal family was taken care of by 22 cooking departments that were staffed by 208 officials and 2124 workers. Work was divided into details in the large departments. There were also specific rules on what the emperor, dukes, senior officials, and scholars should eat during a banquet. The rules also governed the number of dishes, the types of flavourings, cutlery, protocol, music, and songs. There was even a food clinic that specialised in nutritional health and diet treatments.

In the old days, there were strict classifications on the types of dishes one could eat, especially in formal occasions, where dining freedom was severely restricted. The emperor could eat beef, mutton, and pork; dukes could eat beef; ministers could eat mutton; senior officials could eat pork; scholars could eat dried fish; and commoners could eat only vegetables. As the seniority and age increased, the number of dishes would also increase and become more exquisite.

The Evolution of Chinese Eating Practices

Before the Western Han period, the Chinese did not have tables and chairs but sat on floor mats to have their meals. At that time, they would lay floor mats (*yan*), measuring 1 *zhang* (3.3m) each, across the entire room. Straw mats (*xi*) were then laid over the floor mats.

The floor mats were usually made of bamboo or reeds. During banquets, food would be placed on the straw mats and the people would sit on the mats to take their meals.

The terms *yanxi* (feast), *jiuxi* (banquet) and *xiwei* (seat at a conference) were derived from the floor mat.

Proper etiquette in taking one's seat was required. As in kneeling, one's buttocks had to rest on the heels. As the dishes were placed on the floor, one had to bend down to eat. Hence, most of the serving dishes had high stands for greater convenience.

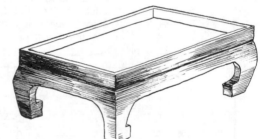

Later on, the serving tray was invented. The serving trays were short and lightweight, and food was placed on them during mealtimes.

The little serving tray complemented the individual serving system where one person had one table to himself. This system was adopted by the Koreans and Japanese. It is common to find such meal practices in Japanese society today.

Similar to the Chinese, the Japanese eat rice with chopsticks but do not drink soup with spoons. Instead, they drink their soup straight from the bowl.

From the Eastern Han period to the Sui and Tang Dynasties, the Chinese switched to having their meals on "beds". Ancient "beds" were low and very different from the type of beds we sleep on today. The same kneeling position was used on the low bed.

Eating on both the mat and low bed resulted in cramped legs and bent backs, which were quite uncomfortable. Hence, eating habits were changed when furniture that followed the natural posture of humans were invented. Soon, chairs, stools and tables were born. From the time of the Tang and Song Dynasties, the people used tables and chairs for eating their meals. The tables and chairs were mostly rectangular and had shorter legs than those used now. Tables and chairs were considered luxury items back in those times and ordinary folks could not afford them. It was not until the Southern Song period that tables and chairs became common furniture.

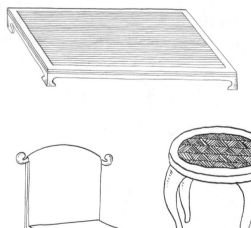

Tao Tie is a term for gluttons. It is also a ferocious mythical creature with a voracious appetite. Some bronze ornaments from the Shang and Zhou Dynasties bear engravings of the creature.

Su Dongpo, the famous literary scholar and food connoisseur of the Song Dynasty once mocked himself with the term *lao tao* (Old Glutton). The renowned Chinese dish "Dongpo Meat" was invented by Su Dongpo.

The Kitchen Lady

It's usually the women who stay home and cook, even though most professional chefs now are men. Female chefs, however, actually came on the scene during the Song Dynasty. Called Kitchen Ladies, they even outranked male chefs, and were more highly paid too. Feted by the royalty, the aristocrats, the rich, and the scholars, they were invited to cook at their homes whenever there was a banquet. Owing to demand, there were even express kitchen lady courses that taught prospective ladies culinary techniques, elegant conduct, and waitressing skills. However, this trade faded away during the later years of the dynasty.

Some kitchen ladies commanded enormous respect, almost like a general! Wow!

The Kitchen Lady who directed the thousand-guest banquet

Wang Zeng, the prime minister during the Song Dynasty, once threw a banquet to commend the officials who had served well. He invited the famed kitchen lady Song Sanniang to be the kitchen director. She arrived with 80 cooks, and proceeded to setting up the cooking utensils and preparing the ingredients — beef, pork, chicken, and vegetables. On the day of the feast, Song Sanniang was all dressed up. Sitting on the stage, she was flanked by two maids who passed on her orders. On her table were flags of various colours — red, blue, yellow, purple, and white. Standing by at the stoves — divided into steaming, roasting, stewing, boiling, and stir-fry — were cooks dressed in corresponding colours. Under the flags and orders of Song Sanniang, the banquet proceeded smoothly.

Chef Ding Analyses the Cow

Brilliant! Brilliant!

I did not expect your skills to have attained this high a level.

During the Warring States period, famous philosopher Zhuang Zi told a fable about a chef.

Your Highness, I do not use skill but feeling when I butcher a cow.

There was once a chef named Ding who slaughtered cows for the king. His technique was flawless.

When I first slaughtered a cow, all I saw was a cow.

Three years later, I only see the anatomy of the cow. Now when I butcher a cow, I need only work by feel.

Cooking Utensils

Chinese Wok *guo*

The wok is the most important utensil in Chinese cooking. From the Han Dynasty to the present, raw iron has been used to manufacture steel woks. The wok has a round or flat bottom, making it suitable for all methods of cooking such as deep-frying, stir-frying, boiling, steaming, roasting or sautéing.

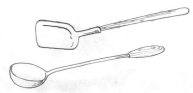

Using the wok to cook is good for the health. It can prevent iron deficiency and the World Health Organisation has encouraged people to cook with woks.

Wok Spatula

Used to stir food in a wok.

Cleaver or Chopper

Chinese dishes demand good knife techniques. A good cleaver is necessary.

Chopping board

A wooden board for cutting food.

Long chopsticks

Can be used to toss food in the wok or move food to a plate.

Sieve

Round bottomed, with many tiny holes for filtering away oil or moisture.

Bamboo steamer

A utensil made of thin bamboo strips and wooden pieces for steaming food.

Claypot

A pot made from potter's clay and sand. Not susceptible to chemical reactions and usually used for stewing food.

Stove

The stove is for starting a fire to prepare food. Most families today have gas stoves at home. In the past, most had brick stoves where wood or charcoal was used to start a fire.

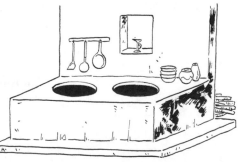

Praying to the Kitchen God

Many people follow the custom of praying to the Kitchen God. The Kitchen God not only controls food and beverage issues, he also records the good and evil deeds that the family has committed and reports them to the Jade Emperor. The Jade Emperor would then reward or mete out punishment to the family,

based on the Kitchen God's report. According to legend, those who committed very evil deeds had their lives shortened by 300 days. Lesser ones got three days taken from their life spans. To get the Kitchen God to say good things about the family, people would offer candied melon to him every 23rd day of the 12th lunar month. With his mouth stuffed with candy, the Kitchen God would not be able to spout bad news and would say only sweet things about the family.

Legend has it that the Kitchen God used to be a poor man by the name of Zhang.

He was a farmer and had a wife who wove cloth. There was a time when a drought hit the area for several years, followed by years of flooding.

Dear wife, you will suffer if you follow me. I will write a divorce petition.

Go back to your parents!

However, Zhang's luck did not change and he lived in great poverty.

CHARACTERISTICS OF CHINESE CUISINE

Colour, smell and taste are the key elements of Chinese cuisine. Chinese food must not only taste good, their apearance must also excite the appetite. With the myriad cooking techniques available, the same ingredients can be made to taste completely different.

Chinese Cuisine Emphasises the Colour, Smell, and Taste of the Dishes

五色 五香 五味

Colour, smell and taste are further divided into five colours, five smells, and five tastes.

The five colours are red, yellow, blue, white, and black. These are the primary colours; the others are the secondary colours. The hues of the dish will determine one's appetite, that's why Chinese dishes favour bright, harmonious and pleasing colours.

五色

The five smells, which mean the five spices, are fennel, chilli, aniseed, Chinese cinnamon, and clove. These spices can make the dish fragrant and whet one's appetite by removing any fishy smell, pungent smell, or mutton smell.

五香

The five tastes are sweet, sour, bitter, hot, and salty. These five basic tastes can also be combined to create composite tastes, such as sweet and salty, hot and sour, numbing hot, or fragrant and hot.

五味

Knife Skills

Your skill in handling the knife is important too. Watch carefully.

Master, that's amazing! I can see that you've applied different techniques.

That's right. Techniques are as important to a cook using his knife as they are to a warrior using his sword. There are endless ways of doing it; you can cut straight down, from the side, or at an angle, mince, chop, slice, pick, knock, or scrape with your knife.

Not only does the knife affect how the dishes look, the thickness of the slices and the size of the cubes will also determine how the food tastes.

The Strength of the Fire

The 18 Skills

Wow! Master, that's amazing!

Actually, there are more than 18 techniques. These are some of the more common ones.

Steam

Place all ingredients in a steamer or wok and make use of the steam from the boiling water to cook the ingredients till done. This method not only allow the food to remain fresh and tender, its nutrients are not easily lost too.

Double-Boil

Put all ingredients in a stewing container, cover and place in a wok or steamer. Allow the steam to cook the ingredients in the container. The cover to the steamer must be kept closed at all times to prevent steam from escaping. Stewed dishes are especially tasty.

Stew in Soy Sauce

To make the stewing gravy, place some spices in a muslin bag, add the bag to a pot of water together with raw ingredients, wine, soy sauce, salt and sugar. Cook over a slow fire till fragrant. After which, place meat into the gravy and cook over a slow flame till soft.

Poach
Cook the food in boiling water.

Stir-fry
Toss the food in the wok quickly. In the process, the ingredients are kept in constant motion. This method enables meat to retain its juices and flavour, and vegetables to remain tender and crisp.

Shallow Fry or Pan-fry
Add a little oil to the pan and fry the food on both sides over moderate heat. When ingredients have turned golden brown, add in flavouring agents and flip the food a few times. Remove from heat when liquid has evaporated.

Deep-fry
The food is cooked in a pot of hot oil. The amount of oil must be substantial and well heated. Before cooking, the ingredients have to be marinated and dipped in batter. Fried foods are tender on the inside and crispy on the outside. Delicious indeed.

Quick-fry

Run ingredients in hot oil or water. Dishes will remain fresh, crisp and tender.

Stew after Frying

In a heated wok, add some oil and stir-fry the ingredients. Add a little water to the wok and bring to boil. Lower the heat and stew till done. After which, turn up the flame and boil off excess liquid.

Sauté

After deep frying, steaming or boiling the food, return it to the wok and toss quickly. Add in seasonings and cornstarch solution such that the gravy bonds to the main ingredient. This method allows the food to maintain its succulence and crunch.

Braise

Briefly cook the meat in hot oil or water, then place it in a pot with some water or thick stock before adding side ingredients. Bring to boil and add some cornstarch solution to thicken the gravy. This method is suitable for cooking fish, prawns, shredded meat and meat slices.

The Seven Daily Necessities

There is a common saying "Seven things meet your eyes when you open the door." They are firewood, rice, oil, salt, soya sauce, vinegar and tea. These are the seven basic necessities.

Cooking oil
In the old days, cooking oil was known as *gao zhi*. *Gao* is melted oil, or grease; and *zhi* is solidified oil, or fat. Oil was used in cooking as early as the Shang and Zhou Dynasties. The earliest oil used was animal fat. During the Han Dynasty, vegetable oil was extracted by crushing fruit kernels.

Soya sauce
The Chinese had mastered the art of making soya sauce about 2,500 years ago. Made from soya beans or broad beans, it adds tastes to dishes.

Firewood
It was only after the discovery of fire that people stopped eating raw food and started the culture of cooking. This is why firewood is considered the foremost necessity in life.

Salt
In ancient times, salt was obtained by boiling off seawater. It is an important seasoning as it helps digestion and adds flavours to the dishes.

Tea
China is the earliest country in the world to cultivate, process, and drink tea. Tea is thirst-quenching and invigorating. It was first used as a medicine, and because of its aroma, eventually became an everyday drink.

Vinegar
The noblemen of the old days used this sour seasoning to ease the fattiness in their meaty feasts and to aid digestion.

Rice
Chinese eat white rice together with other dishes. While one may get bored with even the most delicious dishes if taken everyday, the plain white rice is indispensable to every meal.

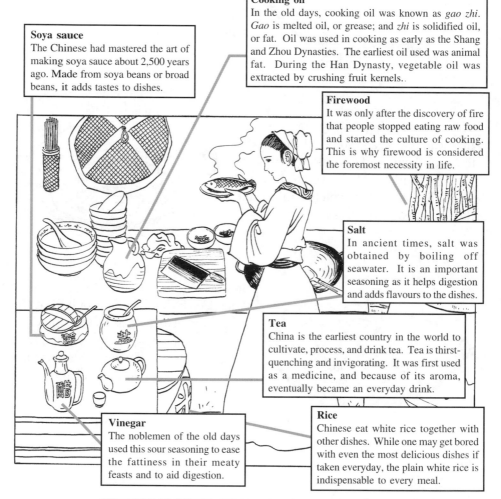

'Eating vinegar' also means 'being jealous'; and a 'vinegar jar' is somebody who gets jealous easily. These seven necessities are all related to food and among them, salt, soya sauce and vinegar are must-haves for every Chinese kitchen.

The Story of Salt

To seek immortality, Emperor Qin Shi Huang went around looking for deities and priests.

Your Majesty, I can show you around the Heavenly Palace.

Stop! Put back the things that you have stolen!

Your Majesty! What did you steal?

In panic, Emperor Qin Shi Huang spilled the salt hidden in his sleeve. At that time, they were crossing the Sea of Japan. Most of the salt fell into the sea while a small portion fell onto the land and lake.

After they returned to the palace, Emperor Qin Shi Huang could not forget the salty salt (*xian yan*) and named the capital "Xian Yan City". It later became known as "Xian Yang City".

The search for salt continued even after Emperor Qin's death. They finally found salt in the sea and sand. From then on, salt became a staple in cooking, enhancing the flavour of dishes.

The Origins of Vinegar

Among seven most important daily necessities, vinegar is an indispensable seasoning in Chinese cooking. It's said that vinegar was discovered accidentally by Du Yu, the son of Du Kang.

Is Du Kang at home?

My dad has gone out. Can I help you?

The emperor would like to try some of his wines. Since you're his son, you'll do too.

Please come with me to the palace.

You're the son of Du Kang? You must know how to brew wine too then.

Your Highness, my father didn't teach me how to brew wine, but I can try.

Du Yu put some distiller's grains in a crock, and covered it with a wooden lid.

Spices Used in Chinese Cuisine

Spices are an integral part of Chinese cuisine. Besides adding flavours, some of them can also be used in healthcare. Here are some of the common spices in Chinese cooking.

Garlic

This fragrant and hot spice can be eaten raw. It can treat malfunctioning organs, prevent influenza, and promote bowel movement. Garlic is commonly used in vinegar sauce, soup, and vegetable, bean curd, meat, and stewed dishes.

Ginger

It can remove the raw mutton or fish smell, promote blood flow, remove toxins, and help digestion. There are old ginger, young ginger, and powder ginger. Old ginger is used in big pieces in *shao* (stewing and then frying) and boiled dishes, or dishes with thick gravy. Powder ginger is prepared in pieces or shreds and used in dishes that are stir-fried quickly.

Pepper

It can remove the meaty taste, bring out the flavour, add to the fragrance, and whet one's appetite. Pepper also reduces chill, relieves pain, clears the phlegm, and induces perspiration. It is suitable for all kinds of dishes, be it hot or cold.

Chilli

This spice is rich in vitamins A and C. It increases one's appetite and reduces rheumatism. Chilli is commonly used in appetisers, soups, and seafood dishes.

Chinese love hot and spicy food. This is especially so in the regions of Yunnan, Guizhou, Hunan, Hubei, Sichuan, Jiangxi, and Shanxi. There is a saying, in Sichuan, the people are *"la bu pa"* (not afraid of hot food); in Hunan they are *"pa bu la"* (afraid that the food is not hot); and in Jiangxi they are *"bu pa la"* (not afraid of hot food).

People in Shanxi eat their *mantou* (bun) with chilli. And in Hainan they even add salt and chilli powder to their watermelon, creating a taste that is sweet, salty and hot at the same time. For the Yunnan people, chilli alone is not hot enough. They will add to it mustard, peppercorn, and garlic paste.

Wow, watermelon, with chilli, dare you try it?

THE ART AND ETIQUETTE OF DINING

In ancient China, not only must food be excellent in taste, aroma and colour, it must also be served in beautiful containers.

Confucius' Discourses On Food

Confucius once said: "Food can never be too refined, meat can never be sliced too thin."

This saying aptly shows that the pursuit of excellence is the essence of Chinese cuisine.

Confucius' eight don'ts of eating:

1. Don't eat fish that is rotten.
2. Don't eat food which has its colour turned bad.
3. Don't eat food that smells bad.
4. Don't eat food that is not well cooked.
5. Don't eat when it is not yet time.
6. Don't eat meat that is not properly cut.
7. Don't eat when the sauce and other seasonings are not properly used.
8. Don't eat wine and dried meat bought from the market.

The Art of Dining in China

Beautiful Utensils for Delicious Food

Good food must be matched with lovely utensils to be perfect!

Olden porcelain serving dishes were adorned with intricate paintings of fishes, birds and other designs.

During the Shang and Zhou Dynasties, the bronze wares had dignified carvings.

Han Dynasty utensils were exquisite works of art.

The silver and golden utensils of the Tang Dynasty were luxurious.

Song Dynasty porcelain was simple yet graceful.

Ming Dynasty teapots, cups and bowls were elegant and practical.

Much thought went into matching the dish with the serving dishes. For example, cold dishes or summer cuisines were usually served in containers that had cool colours (blue, green or azure). Hot food, winter meals or celebratory dishes were served in warm coloured containers (red, orange or yellow).

The colour of the food should not be too similar to the colour of the dish. For example, green vegetables should not be placed on a green plate, as the colour of the vegetables would not stand out.

What a feast! Just the sight is enough to make my mouth water.

Stir-fried dishes should be served on a platter, while soup should be served in a bowl. A beautiful arrangement of small and large dishes on a banquet table will give pleasure to the eye and mind.

Naming Chinese Dishes

Delicious dishes needed delicious names as well. A good dish, if given a beautiful name, would tease the appetite. On the other hand, if the name was ordinary, a good dish would lose its worth. Hence, like naming people, effort needs to go into naming dishes.

Bean sprouts can be called "dragon's beard."

Beancurd can be referred to as "white jade."

Egg becomes "lotus."

Come! Try my dragon's beard, white jade, phoenix claws and lotus! Isn't it magnificent?

What? They're just bean sprouts, bean curd, chicken claws and egg! You miser!

Chicken claws are known as "phoenix's claws."

Among the people, it is common for them to name dishes using auspicious words.

Bamboo shoots fried with spare ribs would be called *bu bu gao sheng* (rising in steps).

Black moss stewed with pig's trotters would be known as *fa cai dao shou* (wealth in the hands).

There were also poetic names such as *ta xue xun mei* (stepping on snow to locate plums) for red peppers with carrot strips.

Sugared tomatoes were called "snow-capped volcano".

There were dishes named after deities and mythical creatures such as the dragon and phoenix. They include *shen xian zhou* (deity porridge), *shen xian tang* (deity soup), *long feng cheng xiang* (brilliance of dragon and phoenix) and *long feng shang yue* (dragon and phoenix admiring the moon).

Some dishes were given names to remember a famous person, for example, *dongpo zhou zi* (Su Dongpo's leg of pork), *ba wang bie ji* (King Chu bids farewell to his concubine), and *gui fei chu yu* (Yang Gui Fei emerges from her bath).

There's also a kind of dish in Chinese cuisine that's made only for viewing, and it comes with very high artistic standards.

Chinese cuisine emphasises presentation

In ancient times, there were *kancai* (viewing dishes), which were made only for presentation and not for eating. Later, grand banquets were even divided into dining area and viewing area. Some dishes at the viewing area were made of flour and purely for show. More ornamental decorations would come with figurines made of clay or coloured dough.

Handicraft dishes

These are edible dishes that are meticulously crafted to look like figurines, flowers, birds, or animals. They are pleasing to the palate as well as the eye, and are very popular in grand banquets.

Design platter

This colourful platter is formed by arranging food items in accordance to their colours and shapes. For example, in a cold platter, Chinese sausage, ham, mushrooms, cucumber, pineapple, cherry and other foods are used to form patterns such as 'fortune brought by the dragon and the phoenix', 'a peacock spreading its tail', and 'twin colourful butterfly'.

Food Taboos

There are many old wives' tales that speak of taboos on food items. Some common ones include:

Young children should not eat chicken claws as it was believed that they would not be able to write well when they went to school. Some believed that children who eat chicken claws would get into fights like roosters.

In olden times, people refrained from eating beef. The reason was because buffaloes had a big role in the agricultural society of yesteryear. These buffaloes had great contributions to mankind and were indispensable to many farmers. Hence, many could not bear to eat beef.

Some places frowned on girls eating pig's trotters. They believed that the girls would not be able to find husbands, or the marriage would be crushed by the trotters.

When eating crabs, it is a taboo to eat one with a missing leg or eye, or one with hair on its stomach.

During wedding banquets, there must an even number of dishes served as good things come in pairs. As for funeral wakes, dishes served must not be in even numbers so that bad things only come once.

In some places in the south of China, steaming New Year cakes is a grand affair because New Year cakes are associated with the term "advancing steadily". Spoiling the cakes would affect the career prospects that year. When steaming the New Year cakes, they are most afraid of children standing nearby who may say something wrong during the process. It is believed that the New Year cakes would not rise if the children interrupt.

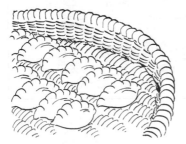

Dumplings are required during the Chinese New Year season. When wrapping dumplings, it is a taboo to arrange the dumplings in a circle. This meant the days in the year would be locked and narrow. Hence, dumplings must be placed in horizontal lines to wish for smooth sailing days ahead and an unobstructed road to riches.

Taboos of Eating

Three Meals A Day

How did the custom of eating breakfast, lunch, and dinner come about? Before the Qin Dynasty, people ate only two meals a day. The rules were strict and it was considered rude to eat at the wrong hour or have more than two meals a day. After the Han Dynasty, it became popular to have three or four meals a day. Usually, breakfast is simply sesame seed cake, steamed bun, deep-fried dough stick, porridge, soya bean milk, or salted vegetables. Lunch consists of rice, steamed bun, steamed twisted roll, and stir-fried vegetables. Dinner includes steamed buns, dumplings, noodles, pancake, and stir-fried vegetables.

There is a saying: "Eat a healthy breakfast, a full lunch, a light dinner." The three meals in a day divide our nutrient intake into three slots; it is a scientific and logical arrangement. However, people who are busy always eat breakfast and lunch together. This means they eat only two meals a day, and have to take in all the necessary nutrients in these two meals. This may increase the workload of the stomach and cause indigestion.

Origins of "Four Dishes and One Soup"

"Four dishes and one soup" means eating four types of dishes and one bowl of soup for a meal.

The concept of "four dishes and one soup" has a long history and it is believed to be created by Zhu Yuanzhang, the first emperor of the Ming Dynasty.

After Zhu Yuanzhang ascended the throne in AD1368, there was a famine due to natural disasters. The commoners suffered.

The Unique Dining Habits of the Minority Races

China is a multi-racial country. Besides the majority Han, there are many other minority races spread across the country. Owing to the differences in geography, produce, climate, and religion, each race has developed its distinctive dining habits and cooking methods.

The Hui's staple foods include rice and noodles. They eat beef, mutton, chicken, duck, fish, and prawns, but not pork; and they say a prayer before slaughtering the animals.

The Zang (Tibetan) nationality eat mostly highland barley. The grain is roasted and ground into powder to make *zanba,* which is consumed with strong tea, milk tea, or sugar. They use wine to dab the table three times before each meal as an offering to Buddha. They eat with their hands instead of chopsticks, and their cutlery set includes a small knife and a wooden bowl.

The Mongolians rear livestock, and eat a lot of red meat such as beef, sheep mutton, goat mutton, camel meat, and sometimes horsemeat. They also consume dairy products such as yogurt, milk curd, butter, and milk tea --- which is an everyday drink for the Mongolian.

The Uygur's daily diet consists of a wheat bread called *ang*. It comes in different sizes — some as big as a washbasin and is normally consumed with mutton soup. Mutton with rice is another delicacy. The Uygur cut their fingernails before dining.

The Man eat a food called *bobo*, which is made from wheat. There are many kinds of *bobo*, and their preparation method varies with the season. They also enjoy eating *furou* — white meat cooked in water.

The Miao's staple is glutinous rice. To them the rice cake is a sign of luck and happiness, and it is indispensable during festive seasons, New Year or wedding celebrations. They love hot and sour food, and each household has its own earthen jar for preserving food such as vegetable, fish, and poultry in sour flavours.

Chinese Banquet Etiquette

Customs and etiquette are very important when throwing a banquet. During the Zhou Dynasty, the basic etiquette and practices for banquet already were drawn up. Some of the practices can still be seen today. The first step is to issue an invitation card which is actually to express respect to the guest.

The table arrangement is centred around the main table. Guests are carefully ushered to the available tables. The first and second tables are usually reserved for the host and important guests. When there are many tables, table numbers can be given. It is proper etiquette to wait to be seated by the host.

When assigning seats, guests are seated based on their seniority, status, kinship or wealth. This is the most complicated and important part of a banquet. A table usually seats eight, and the seating arrangement would differ between eras and locations. In all, the order of seats should *shang zuo zun dong* (respect both the left and the right), with the most esteemed guest facing the main door.

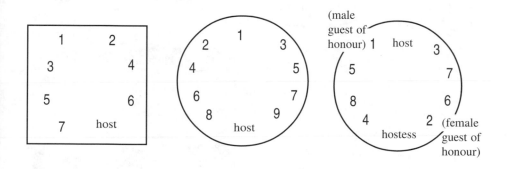

When taking their seats, most guests would give way to one another out of modesty. Hence, it is imperative for the important tables to be filled first before allowing the rest to take their seats.

In ancient times, banquets even featured entertainment such as sword dances, singing, dances, music ensembles, poem recitations or opera performances. The person who served the dishes would usually be the host's maids or juniors. It was common for guests to tip the servers when they brought the main dish. This probably led to the current practice of tipping.

Procedure at a Chinese Banquet

A formal Chinese banquet follows a particular procedure, which is more complicated than a western style buffet.

Several dishes are served at the same time. Each diner is given one bowl and one pair of chopsticks, and they pick whatever dishes they like.

There's a specific sequence in serving. First comes the appetiser (cold dish). At this stage, people can eat, drink, and chat. In big events the host and his guests can give speeches too.

The second course will be a stir-fried dish (a hot dish). The taste now moves from the delicate cold dish to a richer flavour.

The third course will be a *shao* dish (a hot dish), which tastes even heavier. After this dish, the guests can wipe their hands and face with towels and take a break.

The fourth course will be the main dish. This is the climax of the banquet. Guests often toast one another, creating a lively atmosphere. If it is a wedding dinner, the bride and the groom will take this chance to toast the guests.

The fifth course is for the sweeter and lighter tastes of vegetables, soups, desserts, and fruits. This signals the end of the banquet.

The number of courses in a banquet always corresponds to the number of guests at a table, and the portion of each course is more or less similar. Meat and vegetables are often included when preparing the menu. There has to be at least one vegetable and one fish. After serving a hot and spicy dish, the following one has to be light and tasty. Similarly, a sour dish must be matched by a sweeter dish.

A Chinese banquet is also an occasion for socialising. Certain protocols have to be obeyed in order to make the event enjoyable for both the host and the guests.

"Eat slowly" is something people often say at the table. The guests often take their time in sampling the dishes, and consume only moderate portions of each dish.

Have another drink!

The host will always encourage his guests to eat more, and keep serving them wine, rice, and dishes. Before the guest finishes eating, the host will have to stay and eat with the guest even if he's already full.

Thank you!

It's also basic courtesy to help pick up dishes for the guest sitting next to you if he cannot reach it.

Don't try to pick dishes that are far away from you, go rather for the ones nearer to you.

There are normally no small plates to put food remnants or bones. These can be placed next to the bowl.

After each course, one third of the dish would usually be left on the plate. It will be embarrassing for the host if there's nothing left, as he will be seen as a miser.

Please remember all these customs the next time you go to a Chinese banquet.

That's right. This way you can maintain an elegant style while sampling the delicious dishes. That is an art of eating too!

Ancient Picnics

The weather is great today! Most suitable for a picnic!

It seems that people in the olden times already knew how to enjoy having meals in the great outdoors.

They even had special picnic baskets and food warmers. Inside the basket were cutlery, utensils and wine bottles. At the top were compartments which could hold four to six plates.

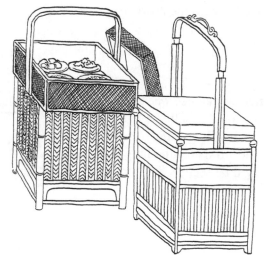

The food warmer had two portions. The top layer was filled with charcoal while the bottom carried a bronze stove. This was used for warming wine. A small pot was also brought along for cooking porridge.

DIET AND HEALTHY LIVING

Food can nourish the body, but a poor diet will cause ill health. The Chinese like to combine foods and medicines as tonics, and even invented many delicious yet healthy foods, like bean curd, porridge, vegetarian dishes and so on.

Food and Health

There's an ancient saying: "Health begins with a healthy diet." Food was considered central to the preservation of health and the treatment of illness. During the Zhou Dynasty, there were 'food physicians', evidence that the earliest medical specialists were dieticians as well. These are the common opinions of ancient doctors in China regarding diet and healthy living.

Have more meals but eat less in each, instead of binging. Strike a balance between hunger and satiation, as overeating increases the workload of the digestive system and hurts digestion.

One should be happy when dining, as anger can affect digestion and cause ill health.

Maintain a balance between the five tastes without having too much of any one. The use of seasonings should be moderated, as an overuse of them can cause sickness.

Eat less meat. Light and delicate food, such as vegetables, is good for digestion and prevents illness.

Practise good hygiene. Wash your hands before eating, and rinse your mouth after meals. A stroll after eating also aids digestion.

The 'eat slowly' habit of the Chinese.

It's common to hear the phrase 'eat slowly' during a Chinese meal. The Chinese have always advised against gulping down food. Instead, they believe that chewing the food slowly is good for health. This is because well-masticated food will provide mild stimulation to the stomach, pancreas, and gall bladder, which is good for the digestion and absorption of nutrients. Chewing also exercises the facial muscles and bones, stimulates facial blood circulation, and works out and strengthens the teeth.

Tonics

Besides the daily food, Chinese also like to use various herbal medicines to make tonic soups. Tonics are for everybody. There's a saying: "If you're sick, the tonic will cure you; if you are not, it will strengthen your body." A typical Chinese is nourished with tonics all his life. Students use it to energise themselves and to promote physical and mental growth. Women take it for one month after giving birth to hasten recuperation. Old folks also need the boost to maintain their aging body.

Tonics are usually double-boiled over a slow fire so as to bring out the active components in the herbs and foods. It is best to use claypots or ceramic utensils to prepare tonics as the ingredients may react with metal pots.

Chinese Medicinal Tonics

Chinese take tonics according to their body types. They believe that as the human body can either be 'hot' or 'cold', so can the food. Those with 'hot' body should eat 'cold' food, and vice versa, in order to restore the balance.

There's a popular saying among the people: one should eat like to nourish like. For example one must eat pig's brain to nourish the brain; and pig's leg to nourish the leg.

Why do you keep eating chicken wings?

I want to grow a pair of wings!

Examples of popular Chinese medicines

Chinese wolfberry
Good for the liver, kidney, blood, and eyes.

Lotus seeds
Nourishes the spleen, stops diarrhoea, and calms the mind.

Black bone chicken
Is considered a kind of Chinese medicine, commonly used in preparing tonics. It nourishes the liver, kidney, blood, and eases asthenic fever.

Food and Tonics for the Seasons

Spring

The weather is warm and windy; therefore the food should be light and delicate. One should eat more vegetables such as bamboo shoots, spinach, and celery; and less fat meat or hot and spicy food. Rain is frequent in spring, which may lead to illnesses such as influenza, skin diseases, fatigue, and lack of appetite. This is a time for tonics that promote growth and nourish the *yang* energy.

Summer

Since the weather is hot, hot and spicy food should be avoided. Instead, eat more light and neutral food, such as bean products, fruits, and vegetables. Raw and cold food should also be avoided as it may upset the stomach. Suitable tonics are those that can reduce heat, such as green bean, Job's tears, tuckahoe, chrysanthemum, honeysuckle, and Chinese wolfberry.

Autumn

The air is dry and one gets tired easily. Food that can nourish the *yin* energy and promote the production of bodily fluids to prevent dryness, such as fruits, vegetables, fish, and egg are most suitable. Common complaints in autumn are chapped lips and skin, constipation, and sore throat. They can be prevented by tonics that nourish the *yin* energy and moisten the body, such as lily, tuckahoe, and dried or prepared rhizome of rehmannia.

Winter

The cold weather increases one's appetite. This is a good time for tonics that are warming and nourishing, such as stewed meat and fish, chafing dish, as well as hot and spicy foods such as chilli, onion, and garlic.

Eat different foods in different seasons. Since most herbal medicines are considered 'hot', people normally consume tonics during winter.

Popular sayings on dining and health

- Don't make noise when you are eating; don't run after a meal.
- Don't chit-chat during a meal.
- Don't binge when you're hungry; don't gulp when you are thirsty.
- Don't shower after a meal.
- Don't rush your meal.
  Avoid drinking tea when the stomach is empty; drinking wine after a meal; and eating rice during dusk.
- Don't eat when you're angry, and don't get angry after a meal.
- Food that tastes good: don't eat too much; food that doesn't: don't eat at all.

Some regions call cooked fish 'the mute dish'. This is to remind people to keep quiet when eating fish, to avoid having a bone stuck in the throat.

Tofu (Bean Curd)

Tofu is a traditional food full of Chinese characteristics; and there is even a tofu cultural festival in China.

The soft, tender, nutritious, and affordable bean curd is a popular everyday food for many.

How tofu is made:

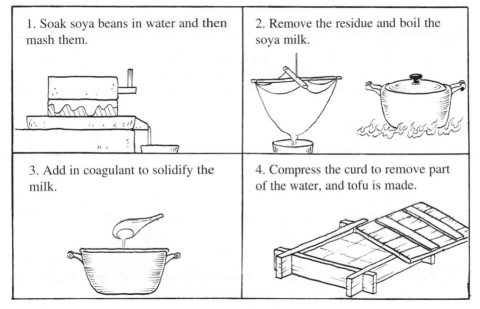

1. Soak soya beans in water and then mash them.	2. Remove the residue and boil the soya milk.
3. Add in coagulant to solidify the milk.	4. Compress the curd to remove part of the water, and tofu is made.

Tofu was originally a food for monks and Taoist priests. It later spread to the public and became a popular delicacy. Tofu has a delicate taste when eaten on its own, but it can also be matched with other ingredients to create many other tofu dishes. It is estimated that there are more than 400 types of tofu dishes, such as the Sichuan Pockmarked Lady's Tofu, the Zhejiang Dongpo Tofu, the Lanxi Five Spices Tofu, and the Jiangsu Eight Treasures Tofu.

Tofu is not only a favourite among the Chinese, but it is also popular in many other countries, such as Japan, the United States, Canada, and Germany. Japanese use vegetable extract to make green tofu, strawberry to make red tofu, and sesame to make beige tofu. Americans like to add other ingredients to the tofu, and create dishes such as tofu roast duck and tofu wedding cake. A US magazine even claimed that tofu from China has more market potential than cars, televisions, or electronics.

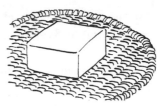

The nutritional value of tofu

There is a Chinese saying: "Vegetables and tofu keep you safe and sound." Tofu has high nutritional values, and is good for one's health.

Tofu can be used to:

Nourish one's *qi*, or energy.
Promote the production of bodily fluid to reduce dryness.
Reduce heat and remove toxins.
Reduce blood cholesterol and the chances of heart diseases; prevent senile dementia and obesity.
Reduce respiratory and digestive problems.

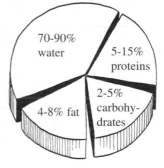

Tofu is good for skincare too. It is said that the beauty-conscious Empress Dowager Cixi insisted on one tofu dish every day.

The royal kitchen had 49 steamers, and inside each was tofu with pearl inlay. The steamers took turns to prepare the dish, so that the empress could have her daily dose of pearly tofu to maintain her looks.

Other tofu-related food items

Dried tofu
Tofu wrapped in cloth and steamed with spices.

Jelly tofu
Half-solidified bean curd made by adding coagulant to soya milk after it is boiled.

Tofu skin
This is the thin layer of skin on top of boiled soya milk, ready to eat once it is air-dried. Also called *qianzhang*.

Fermented tofu
Small pieces of fermented and preserved tofu.

During a Chinese wake, guests are served with rice and vegetarian food, including tofu. It is called a 'tofu meal'.

"Eating somebody's tofu" also means pulling somebody's legs. For example, "He is eating your tofu" means he is joking with you.

The Invention of Tofu

Tofu was said to be invented by Liu An, the emperor of Huan Nan, and who was also the grandson of the Western Han emperor Liu Bang.

In his search for immortality, he experimented with various ingredients to create an elixir.

One day, he put soya milk and bittern together.

Hmm, what is this white and soft thing?

It's delicious!

This 'elixir' is actually tofu. While eating it may not give you eternal life, it is certainly good for your health.

Porridge

This watery rice dish is popular among the Chinese. It is consumed during breakfast by many people, regardless of their social status or geographical region. Legend has it that the Yellow Emperor created the dish. As early as 3,000 years ago, porridge had already been listed as one of the six drinks in the palace. During the Tang Dynasty, porridge was even bestowed by the emperor on his officials as a royal reward.

There are many types of porridge. *The Porridge Guide* from the Qing Dynasty listed six categories — grain, vegetable, fruit, plant, medicinal, and meat, and 240 types of porridge. Not only does porridge fill the stomach, it's nourishing too. In his *Compendium of Materia Medica,* Li Shizhen, a famed doctor during the Ming Dynasty, recorded 36 kinds of porridge. He also noted the watery dish's efficacy in nourishing the spleen, increasing appetite, promoting vitality, soothing the nerves, cleansing the heart, and enriching the blood. There was also medicinal porridge, where medicines and grains were cooked together. Not only did it cure and prevent illnesses, it also promoted longevity.

Tonic porridges

Ingredients	Usage
White lotus seed	treats insomnia
Chrysanthemum	reduces heat and brightens the eye
Red date	good for skincare
Chinese yam	treats shortness of breath and body weakness
Haw	treats indigestion and clears blood clots
Sugar cane	reduces heat, moistens dryness and nourishes the *qi*, or energy
Peanut coat	nourishes the blood platelets
Longan	treats deficiency of the heart and lack of *qi*
Lychee	nourishes the kidney, spleen, and blood
Arillus longan	nourishes the heart, spleen, blood, and calms the mind
Reed rhizome	reduces high fever
Carrot	cures headache and high blood pressure
Chinese wolfberry	nourishes the liver, kidney, blood and eyes
Kiwi fruit	quenches thirst and cures dysphoria
Sweet rice (glutinous rice)	prevents and cures athlete's foot
Walnut	nourishes the kidney, lung, spleen, and stomach
Job's tears	cures dizziness and profuse perspiration
Lotus rhizome	cures constipation and nourishes the *qi*
Lotus leaf	prevents heat stroke
Chestnut	nourishes the kidney, waist, knee, *qi*, spleen, and stomach
Monkshood	nourishes the spleen, the *yang* energy, reduces cold and pain
Sesame	nourishes the liver, kidney, spleen, stomach, and moistens the intestine
Pine nut	moistens the lung, stops coughing, and relaxes the bowel
Groundnut	nourishes the *qi*, blood, lungs, and stops coughing
Lotus root	nourishes the *qi*, blood, spleen, and promotes appetite
Green bean	reduces heat and swelling, removes toxins

La Ba Porridge

Every year on the eighth (*ba*) day of the twelfth lunar month (*la*), people would cook *La Ba* porridge as an offering to the ancestors and Buddha. After the prayer, the porridge would be distributed to relatives and friends and be eaten together by the whole family. This is to give thanks to Heaven for its blessings and to pray for a bountiful harvest. Not only is it consumed by humans, it's fed to the livestock and house pets as well. It was also smeared on walls and trees around the house. *La Ba* porridge is known as the King of Porridge in China. It's prepared with rich ingredients, such as white rice, glutinous rice, coarse rice, millet, Job's tears, sorghum, peas, water chestnut seeds, red beans, green beans, soybeans, red dates, lotus seeds, walnut seeds, peanuts, longan, melon seeds, raisins, vegetable slices, and dried orange peels. Grains and fruits from the fields, the orchards, and the hills are all ingredients for the porridge.

La Yue is the twelfth lunar month that marks the transition between the end of winter and the beginning of spring. It is also the time when harvest is completed and the farm is idle. People would go hunting in the wild, and offer the kill as sacrifice to their ancestors and the gods on the eighth day of the month, in order to pray for longevity, prosperity, and good fortune. This is called *La Ji* (offerings in the twelfth month). The eighth day of the twelfth month is also said to be the day Sakyamuni, the founder of Buddhism, attained his enlightenment. Therefore it's also widely celebrated by the Buddhists. The custom of eating *La Ba* Porridge on *La Ba* day started during the Song Dynasty, and has been in practice for more than 1,000 years. People also make cured pork and mutton, called *la rou* or *la wei*, for the upcoming Lunar New Year celebrations.

The Story of *La Ba* Porridge 2

It's said that Sakyamuni was a prince before he attained enlightenment. He travelled all over India, seeking out wise men, talking to strangers, and cultivating hard, trying to find the meaning of life.

One day, He arrived at the Magadha kingdom in northern India.

Are you all right?

I'm hungry and thirsty.

I have some mixed grains. Please wait a while.

Soup

Soup is indispensable to every Chinese meal. It has a long history that goes back over 7,000 years.

The benefits of drinking soup:

A few gulps of soup can ease the swallowing of food.

Drinking soup during meals can dilute the food and help digestion.

Drinking soup prevents weight gain too — a bowl of soup before a meal can prevent over-eating, and reduce the energy intake of that meal.

The Chinese drink tonic soups that are prepared with various types of medicines. They are very nutritious! The Cantonese particularly are fond of cooking soups.

Tonic soups are normally prepared by cooking meat or eggs together with medicines and other ingredients. They are delicious and nutritious.

The medicinal values of various soups:

Rib soup: promotes the growth of bones.

Chicken soup: strengthens the body and prevents influenza and tracheitis.

Fish soup: prevents asthma and inflammation of the respiratory tract.

Kelp soup: promotes blood circulation and strengthens the body against chill.

Vegetable soup: cleanses the toxins in the body.

Chinese Vegetarian Food

Vegetarian food is a distinctive feature of the Chinese culinary scene. The cuisine is characterised by its specific ingredients, refined preparations and meticulous cooking. The dishes come in unique colours, smells, tastes, and shapes, earning them the admirations of many.

Vegetarian food had been around before Buddhism reached China during the Eastern Han Dynasty; and became more popular after the religion's arrival.

The kitchen in the temple is called *zhai chu,* or vegetarian kitchen. Besides taking care of the monks' meals, it also caters to the visiting monks. Popular temples receive many guests and pilgrims throughout the year. Serving so many of them has prompted the kitchens to be more particular in their vegetarian cooking.

The main ingredients in vegetarian food are mushrooms, fungi, fruits, vegetables, flowers, and bean products. The items may be basic, but great skills are needed in the preparations. Out of these ingredients can come chicken, duck, fish, and ham. Not only do they look like the real thing, they taste like it as well. "A gourd can become tens of dishes; a dish can have tens of tastes," so goes the saying.

Of all the vegetarian dishes in the temple, *Luo Han Zhai* is the main item. It is made of 18 ingredients, as a reference to the 18 *luo han* (or arhat) in Buddhism. The dish spread from temples to vegetarian restaurants, and was further improved to become a delicacy that is loved by all.

LOCAL SNACKS

In China, there is a great variety of local delights that have significantly enriched the gastronomic scene of China, such as deep-fried dough stick, porridge, fermented bean curd, steamed bun, and stuffed bun. These snacks, created through the ingenuity and hard work of the local people, have brought delight to generations of people.

Cakes

There are more than 1,000 types of cakes in China. It was said that cake was first made over 2,000 years ago during the Shang and Zhou Dynasties.

Chinese cakes are always adorned with patterns. The designs are engraved on wooden moulds, which are then pressed on to the surface of the cake. The popular red turtle cake has a turtle shell pattern that symbolises longevity.

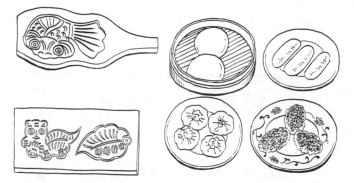

Cakes are also called *dian xin*, or dim sum. Cantonese like to visit teahouses to drink tea and eat dim sum. Delicacies such as *xiaolongbao*, *shaomai*, and prawn rolls are served around the tables on pushcarts by waiters.

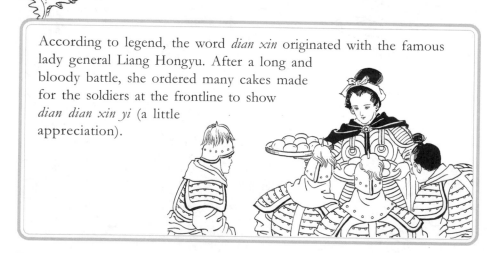

According to legend, the word *dian xin* originated with the famous lady general Liang Hongyu. After a long and bloody battle, she ordered many cakes made for the soldiers at the frontline to show *dian dian xin yi* (a little appreciation).

The First Cakes

In the late Shang Dynasty, the emperor sent WenTaishi to war.

Preparing meals take too long.

Wen Taishi ordered that flour and sugar be made into bars for travel food.

Let the troops eat this as they march.

It is indeed much faster.

Later, the common people made different types of cakes based on the sweet biscuits. Wen Taishi thus became the originator of the confectionery trade.

Youtiao (deep-fried dough stick)

This is a traditional Chinese snack, made from deep-fried dough and served during breakfast. It is normally served with pancakes, rice, or porridge. It's said that *youtiao* was first made in Hangzhou during the Southern Song dynasty. When it spread overseas, foreigners took up eating the snack as well. It can now be found in the United States, Japan, the Philippines, and Spain. *Youtiao* looks simple, but it's actually complicated and difficult to make. During summer, to avoid the fermenting dough becoming too alkaline or acidic, one has to stay up all night to knead the dough to get the best quality.

The Story of *Youtiao*

Yue Fei gallantly led the Song army to repel the Jin invaders. This won him the support of the people.

In 1142, the treacherous Prime Minister Qin Hui, who ruled tyrannically with his wife, Wang Shi, executed Yue Fei without providing any reasons.

The lackeys of Qin Hui… I'd better watch my tongue.

Wouldn't it be great if I can fry that treacherous Qin Hui in hot oil?

That's it! I'll make a Qin Hui with my dough!

Smelly Bean Curd

This is a unique Chinese dish that has a special fragrance amidst its strong smell.

On the bean curd grows a mould that produces the enzyme protease, which breaks down protein into amino acids and gives the bean curd its distinctive taste.

Some like to eat smelly bean curd with brown peppercorn oil or sesame oil; and others like to deep-fry the bean curd with red chilli to give more spice to its flavour.

Smelly bean curd has high nutritional value — two pieces of it contain as much protein as an egg. And because it's fermented by micro-organisms, its nutrients can be more readily digested and absorbed by the human body. Of all smelly bean curds, the Wang Zhihe smelly bean curd in Beijing is the most famous.

The Story of Beijing Smelly Bean Curd

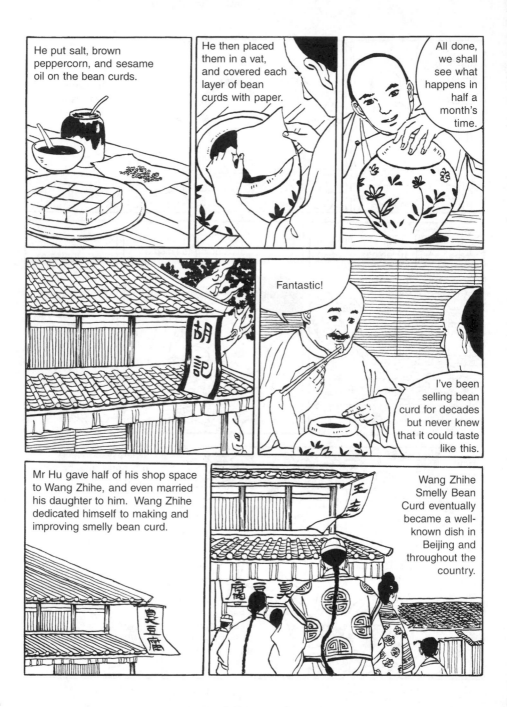

He put salt, brown peppercorn, and sesame oil on the bean curds.

He then placed them in a vat, and covered each layer of bean curds with paper.

All done, we shall see what happens in half a month's time.

Fantastic!

I've been selling bean curd for decades but never knew that it could taste like this.

Mr Hu gave half of his shop space to Wang Zhihe, and even married his daughter to him. Wang Zhihe dedicated himself to making and improving smelly bean curd.

Wang Zhihe Smelly Bean Curd eventually became a well-known dish in Beijing and throughout the country.

Mantou (steamed bun)

This snack is made from steamed fermented flour. It's said that Zhuge Liang, a famous strategist from the Three Kingdoms period, first created it.

At first *mantous* were as big as a human head and had meat fillings. They were used as decorations during banquets and offering ceremonies.

After the Tang and Song Dynasties, *mantou* gradually became a dessert, and its size got smaller too.

Later, mantous without fillings were made. In order to differentiate the two, those with fillings were called *baozi*, and those without were called *mantou*. There were different kinds of fillings for *baozi*, such as meat, vegetable, bean paste, and lotus paste.

The Story of *Mantou*

During the Three Kingdoms period, the famed military strategist Zhuge Liang led a campaign against Meng Huo of the Man tribe.

Here comes the miasma again.

I heard the Mans practise witchcraft. Do you think this is one of their tricks?

The soldiers are not accustomed to this warm and humid place, and the long journey is also affecting morale.

I heard the Mans can summon the heavenly soldiers to their aid.

Wouldn't it be great if our prime minister can do that too?

Summon the heavenly soldiers? That's easy.

I heard the Mans use human heads as offerings.

Hmm...

Goubuli (ignored by dogs) *Baozi*

Wow! This big bun has thin skin and delicious fillings, and it's rich but not greasy.

Of course. This is the famous *goubuli* bun from Tianjin.

That's a strange name. Why would dogs ignore a bun as delicious as this?

'Ignored by dogs' is actually the nickname of a waiter in the Tongzhi Year during the Qing Dynasty.

Because he was skilled at making buns, people named his buns after him.

The buns are made by a meticulous process. All the ingredients have to be measured accurately with a scale.

Wow, that's a precise process. No wonder it tastes so good.

The proportion of the fillings also changes with the seasons. For example, during summer the ratio of fat to lean meat is 3:7. During winter this will change to 6:4.

Century Egg

Century eggs are made by wrapping duck eggs in mud and salt, then burying them over a long period of time. Once the eggs have become greyish green in colour and unique in taste, they are ready to be eaten.

Century egg is rich in nutrients such as protein, vitamins, fatty acids, and amino acids. Matching it with other ingredients such as lean meat and shrimp will create many unique dishes. Century egg porridge is also another nutritious example.

The Story of the Century Egg

Nobody comes to drink tea because of the rain. We'll have to go hungry.

Once upon a time in Jiangnan, there lived an old couple by the name of Li who ran a tea stall by the river. One year, rain fell for a whole month.

When they lay eggs, you can sell the eggs.

A kind duck-seller gave them two female ducks.

One day, the old lady poured some leftover tea on the ash chamber.

I have reared this pair of ducks for half a month but they haven't laid any eggs!

Ah! The eggs have been buried here!

These eggs were laid half a month ago.

I wonder if the eggs have gone bad after being buried for half a month.

The eggs are fine. They even smell quite fragrant!

This egg can be eaten without cooking.

And it's quite tasty!

The couple sold the rest of the eggs.

Everybody loved the eggs. As the eggs had a texture like leather, they were thus named "leather eggs" in Chinese.

Rock Sugar Bottle Gourd

Rock sugar bottle gourd is a unique roadside snack that is loved by the old and the young alike. However, this sweet and sour snack is actually not made from gourds. Instead, it's prepared by coating balls of haw with rock sugar, and then stringing them together in bamboo skewers. Hawkers pierce the skewers on a bundle of straw, and peddle them around town on their shoulders.

Rock sugar bottle gourd was first used as a medicine as haw helps digestion, clears blood clog, and lowers the cholesterol level. It is indeed a delicious and nutritious snack.

Besides haw, crabapples, Chinese yams, grapes, walnut kernels, apples, pears, and tangerines are also used to make the snack.

Noodles

Besides rice, noodles are also a staple food of the Chinese. In ancient times noodles were called *tangbing* or *butuo*. *Tangbing* is handmade by pressing the dough into thin pieces; and *butuo* is made by cutting the dough into slices with a knife.

In the old days, there would be a *tangbing* party three days after a baby was born, and relatives and friends were invited to eat noodles. Nowadays, Chinese still love to eat noodles during birthdays, because the long and slender noodles signifies longevity in China. It also means wishing somebody a long life.

The making of noodles

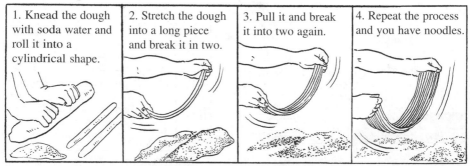

1. Knead the dough with soda water and roll it into a cylindrical shape.	2. Stretch the dough into a long piece and break it in two.	3. Pull it and break it into two again.	4. Repeat the process and you have noodles.

The Five Noodles of China

Shanxi knife-sliced noodles

This noodle is made with a unique process. First, the chef kneads the flour into dough. When the cauldron of water is boiled, he uses a knife to quickly slice the dough into pieces, straight into the boiling water.

Beijing noodles with fried bean sauce

Pour fried bean sauce onto cooked noodles, and add some cucumber and bean sprout shreds. Mix well with chopsticks, and the sweet and spicy noodles are ready to eat.

Shandong Yifu noodles

This deep fried egg noodle dish was created over 300 years ago by the chef of Yi Bingshou in Zhi Fu, Yangzhou. Some say it is the earliest form of instant noodles in the world.

Henan baked fish noodles

Ramen as thin as hair is deep-fried and served with sautéd fish; it has a uniquely delicious taste.

Sichuan *dandan* noodles

It got its name from how it is peddled by hawkers – by carrying it on a shoulder pole (*dan*). On one end of the pole is a stove, and on the other are noodles, bowls, and seasonings. The noodles are thin; the sauce is fragrant and tastes salty and slightly hot.

Guangdong roast pork noodles and Chaozhou fishball noodles are popular too! Chinese noodles are enjoyed all over the world. Ramen, Japan's national dish, is actually Chinese noodles!

The Origins of Ice-Cream

It's so warm. An ice-cream will cool me down.

Adults and children love ice-cream.

But many don't know that ice-cream originated in China!

Really?

In ancient times, to relieve the summer heat, the emperor would make his slaves store winter snow in an underground chamber so that he could enjoy the cool ice during summer.

After which, some traders added sugar, fruits, juices and milk to the ice to attract customers.

In the late Tang Dynasty, people mined the mineral nitre to produce gunpowder. They discovered that nitre caused water to lose heat quickly and become ice. That was how people learnt to make ice during summer.

In the 13th century, the art of making ice-cream was brought to Italy by Marco Polo, and it was subsequently brought to France. The Italians and French improved the method of making ice-cream and added more variety to the dessert, thus making it one of the world's favourite food items.

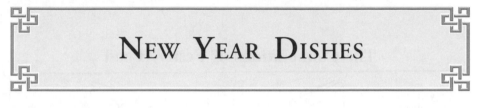

NEW YEAR DISHES

Chinese always prepare special dishes for festive seasons, especially during the Lunar New Year celebrations, where many delicious dishes with auspicious connotations are made.

The Connotations of Festive Food

Do you know the meanings of these festive food items?

Dumplings on New Year's Eve?

They connote 'out with the old and in with the new'.

Soup dumplings on the 15th night of the first lunar month?

They symbolise reunion.

Eating *zongzi* and drinking realgar liquor during the Dragon Boat Festival?

Zongzi is to commemorate the patriotic poet Qu Yuan; realgar liquor is to ward off evil.

Mooncakes during the Mid-autumn Festival?

A mooncake is as round as the moon, it signifies all's well, and the family is reunited.

The Symbolism of New Year Dishes

On New Year's Eve, the whole family would sit down together for a reunion dinner. Dishes at this dinner have special meanings. For example, the whole chicken, duck, or fish must be served, with the head and the tail included.

The dishes are also prepared with ingredients that symbolise prosperity.

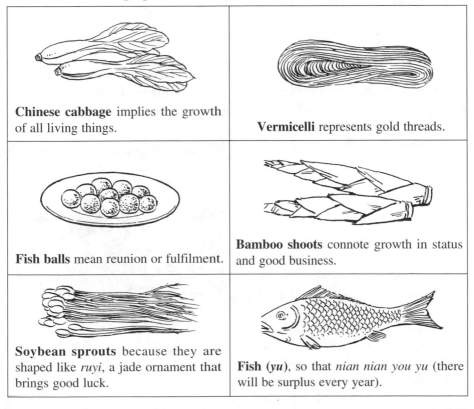

Chinese cabbage implies the growth of all living things.	**Vermicelli** represents gold threads.
Fish balls mean reunion or fulfilment.	**Bamboo shoots** connote growth in status and good business.
Soybean sprouts because they are shaped like *ruyi*, a jade ornament that brings good luck.	**Fish (*yu*)**, so that *nian nian you yu* (there will be surplus every year).

Chafing dish

Many families now like to eat chafing dishes during reunion dinners. This is because it's easy to prepare, rich in ingredients, and is suitable for the young and the old. The dish originated in the Shang and the Zhou Dynasties, but became popular only during the Qing Dynasty. It's not only enjoyed by the commoners, but by the royalty as well. It's said that during the coronation of Emperor Jia Qing during the Qing Dynasty, there was a chafing dish banquet where 1,650 stoves were used.

When eating the dish, the soup in the pot is always boiling, and pieces of meat and vegetable are cooked in the soup. Cantonese call this 'da bian lu', and in the north it's called 'shuan huo guo'. Each region has its own way of cooking, and its own unique set of stoves, ingredients, and sauces. There are also a rich variety of chafing dishes, such as plain pork dish, mixed dish, and Cantonese dish.

Some places are particular about their chafing dishes. For example, when serving guests in the northeast region, fowl such as birds and wild geese are placed at the front of the stove; meat such as venison, pork, beef, and mutton are placed at the back; fish is on the left; and prawns are on the right. The dish

is then topped with assorted shredded vegetables. If the guest is an unwelcome person, two extra large meatballs will be placed at the front, followed by meat at the back. It implies *gun dan* (get lost).

Yuan Shizu and the Chafing Dish

Snacks During the Lunar New Year

Niangao (New Year cake)

It is made by steaming dough made from rice powder. When it is done, it turns golden brown, with a sticky and sweet texture. This *niangao* (sticky cake) later became known as *niangao* (New Year cake). It also means *nian nian gao sheng* (growing in status every year).

Tangyuan

Yuanxiao, or more commonly known as *tangyuan*, are sweet dumplings made from glutinous rice flour. The fillings can be peanuts, red beans, jujube, bamboo shoots, or meat. They are consumed on the 15th day of the first month, and represent reunion and happiness.

Spring rolls

These cylindrical rolls are made by wrapping fillings with dough sheets, and deep-frying them in oil. They symbolise good harvest and prosperity.

The Origin of New Year Cake

Niangao is a popular festive snack that has been around for thousands of years. It's said that the cake originated in Suzhou during the Spring and Autumn period. Suzhou was then the capital city of the Wu kingdom, where its emperor He Lu was assisted by Wu Zixu in administration matters. The country once met with a spell of good weather, which gave it bountiful harvest for several seasons.

We should save the harvest surplus for the rainy days.

Your Highness, please allow me to take care of this matter.

Wu Zixu ordered the excess grains to be immersed in water and steamed.

The grains were then mashed into paste to form bricks.

Stack these rice bricks up along the city wall, and cover them with another layer of brick wall.

After Emperor He Lu died, his son Fu Chai succeeded to the throne. He waged war on the northern states to gain domination, and acting upon slanderous rumours, forced Wu Zixu to commit suicide.

Wu kingdom was later counter-attacked by the Yue kingdom. The resulting political upheaval caused widespread famine.

Dumplings

Dumplings are one of the most representative traditional foods in China. During the fifth century, dumplings were a common dish along the Yellow River valley. In those days, the dumplings were eaten together with the soup they were boiled in and called *huntun* (dumpling soup). During the Tang Dynasty, dumplings were served separately on a plate, and had already taken up the shape that it is in today. Certain regions consume dumplings as breakfast during the first three or five days of the Lunar New Year. This is due to their gold ingot shape, which implies the arrival of fortune. They can also be filled with auspicious ingredients that signify people's New Year wishes. For example, peanuts represent health and longevity, honey and sugar mean better days ahead, and coins or jewelry connote good fortune.

The first dumpling dish has to be prepared by midnight during the New Year's Eve. Care has to be taken when picking up the dumpling, as breaking it would suggest bad luck for the coming year. During the Qing Dynasty, dumplings were also presented as presents to the emperor during his birthday. The preparation method of dumplings is renewed continually, and over 100 types of dumplings can be produced for a 'dumpling feast'.

The Story of Dumplings 1

Qing Taizu, the founder of the Qing Dynasty, was a tramp when he was young.

One New Year's Eve, he passed through a village.

It's so quiet here; there isn't a bit of New Year atmosphere.

Young man, are you mad enough to stay outside at this hour?

Grandpa, I'm from out of town; what's happening here?

There's a man-eating monster called 'mahuzi' in this village.

Those who ventured out were killed; that's why we don't dare to go out anymore.

The Story of Dumplings 2

Eating Customs During the Lunar New Year

According to old customs, one must consume 10 dishes on the first day of the first month. They include *niangao* (New Year cake), spring rolls, steamed sponge cakes, and dumplings. People in certain regions would eat only vegetarian meals on this day.

Dumplings are served on the second day. They are shaped like ancient gold ingots, and are therefore called Fortune God Dumplings.

The third day is for soup dumplings, which are shaped like gold ingots too.

The fourth day is for noodles. The long and slender shape suggests longevity. And because *mian* (noodles) sounds like *mian* (avoid), it can also ward off bad luck.

The fifth day is when people resume eating rice.

On the seventh and eighth days, Chinese in the South East Asia region like to eat 'rainbow *yusheng*'. It's a special dish made of shredded vegetables, carrots, raw fish slices, and topped with sauces. Prior to serving, people would toss the ingredients together with their chopsticks while saying auspicious words.

Toss! Toss! Toss up good fortune and prosperity!

CHOPSTICKS

Chopsticks are distinctively Chinese utensils that have at least 5,000 years of history. Besides its role in dining, a pair of chopsticks also carries many connotations that made it a part of the Chinese culture.

Chopsticks were once called *zhu**.

The Types of Chopsticks and Their Usage

Chopsticks are made from various kinds of materials, such as wood, ivory, jade, gold, and silver. Different materials impart different characteristics to the chopsticks. For example, jade chopsticks don't conduct heat and ivory chopsticks cool the food. Chopsticks are suitable for all kinds of dishes, whether hot or cold, fried, cooked, roasted, or deep-fried. It can also be used to pick up food in slices, small cubes, big chunks, or small pieces.

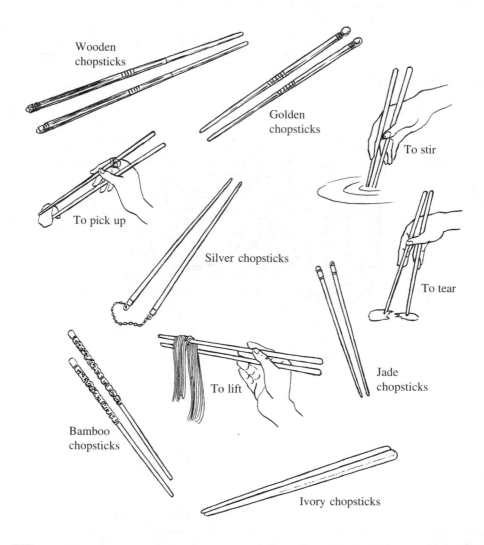

Wooden chopsticks

Golden chopsticks

To stir

To pick up

Silver chopsticks

To tear

To lift

Jade chopsticks

Bamboo chopsticks

Ivory chopsticks

Why Chopsticks?

Although spoons, forks and knives were discovered in archaeological digs, Chinese didn't develop any habit of eating with their bare fingers, or forks and knives.

China is an agricultural society. Since the old days grains like millet and husked rice cooked into rice or porridge have always been the staple food of the people. Using chopsticks to rake the rice or porridge is easier than using a spoon.

Chinese like to eat hot food. That's why they always say, "Please eat while it's still hot". It's inconvenient to take hot oily or soupy food with bare fingers. Furthermore, Chinese cuisine emphasises aesthetics, and bars the use of forks and knives in certain circumstances. That's why the nimble chopsticks were used instead.

The rice bowl is the basic Chinese crockery used to serve dishes and rice. It is not as big as a plate, and is not suitable for forks and knives. A pair of chopsticks, therefore, is a better match for rice bowl.

A rice bowl and a pair of chopsticks are a perfect match!

The development of chopsticks

The primitive forms of chopsticks were bamboo sticks and twigs. By chance, people found that they could use the sticks to pick up food, and modified them for use. In time, the sticks evolved into today's chopsticks.

Chinese started using chopsticks as early as 5,000 years ago. However, in the beginning, spoons were used more often, and chopsticks were only used to pick up food items from the soup. It was not until the 14th century, during the Ming and Qing Dynasties, that chopsticks became popular.

Chopsticks were once called *zhu*. So how did they get to be known as chopsticks? It was said that during the Ming and Qing dynasties, the southern boat dwellers were averse to words that were inauspicious to sailing. *Zhu* sounded like *zhu* (stop), which suggested the ships would not move. So they renamed chopsticks *kuai zi*. *Kuai* is a homophone of *kuai* (fast), which connoted the ships would sail fast.

The History of Chopsticks

The Bamboo Sisters

Long ago, before the invention of chopsticks, people ate rice with hands, cut food with knives, and served dishes with ladles.

At the west bank of Hu'erhan River lived a pair of sisters from the Man tribe. They were skilled at cooking.

Sister, why does the *wulielie* dish smell so good when we are preparing it…

… but tastes like swill when we eat it with a ladle?

I had a dream last night. An old lady with white hair told us to travel 5,000 miles south, and look for a tall, hollow plant with constant diameter, called bamboo.

I dreamt of her too! She said if we used slender sticks made from the bamboo to pick up food, it would preserve the flavour.

She also said that…

It's not easy to find the bamboo. If you are in danger just call 'ya'er hu' three times, and I'll come to your rescue.

Jiang Zi Ya and Chopsticks

Jiang Zi Ya was only discovered by King Zhou Wen at the age of eighty. Before that, he lived a life of poverty with his wife.

I married him because I believed him when he told me how much talent he had. He is already so old, when would he ever establish himself? He has caused me to live the life of a pauper…

Where did you get the meat? It smells delicious!

Aiyah! Get lost!

What's wrong with this bird? Is there something wrong with the meat?

This bird stopped me from eating! I will roast it for food!

The Correct Way of Holding Chopsticks

1. Chopsticks are usually held at mid-length with the right hand. Place one chopstick between the thumb and the index finger, and press the tip of the middle finger against it. This chopstick will remain in place.

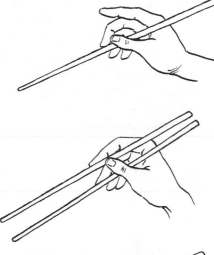

2. Position the second chopstick between the thumb and the tip of the middle finger, and support the upper half with the index finger.

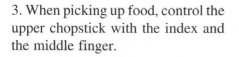
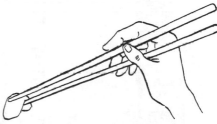

3. When picking up food, control the upper chopstick with the index and the middle finger.

It's said that using chopsticks promotes the development of one's intelligence. This is because using chopsticks involves over 30 joints and 50 muscles in the fingers, wrist, arm, and shoulder, as well as thousands of nerves. The arms are more closely connected to the brains than the other organs. The repetitive motions in using the chopsticks stimulate the mind, and promote the full development of intelligence.

The Art of Chopsticks

Colour, scent and taste have always been important in Chinese cuisine. Excellent food, therefore, must be accompanied by beautiful crockery. As the main utensil, it's no surprise that more and more artistic chopsticks are made. They are usually decorated with drawings of flowers, birds, insects, fish, animals and human figures, or carvings of dragons, phoenixes, unicorns, and lion heads. Sometimes precious metals or stones, such as gold, silver, or pearls, are also used to adorn the sticks.

Various chopstick designs

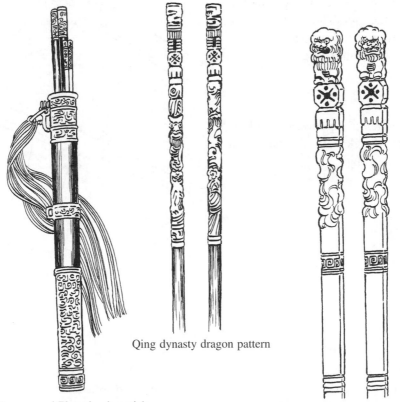

Qing dynasty dragon pattern

Dragon and Phoenix chopsticks

Carved lion-headed chopsticks

How the Use of Chopsticks Was Handed Down

Chopsticks were first used in China, and later in Korea, Japan, and other countries.

The Korean peninsula started dining with chopsticks over 1,000 years ago, making it the first country outside China to use the utensil. When a Korean girl gets married, the dowry must include a pair of silver chopsticks and silver spoons. When a child is born, the mother's parents must send as a gift a set of small chopsticks and spoons engraved with the baby's name.

Japan has its own unique chopstick culture. Not only do the Japanese emphasise the workmanship of the chopsticks, they are also particular about the choice of chopsticks for different occasions. Bamboo chopsticks are used during grand banquets and state ceremonies at peacetime. Willow wood chopsticks are for birthdays and first meals of young children. Dining while admiring the full moon is an occasion for lespedeza wood chopsticks. For offerings, clean wooden chopsticks are the choice.

In certain regions, new chopsticks are used during sowing, transplanting of rice seedlings, and harvesting as a way of celebration. There is even a thanksgiving ceremony in which appreciation is expressed to the chopsticks for their contributions in dining, and to bless the trees and bamboo that have been cut down to make chopsticks. Japan has also designated 4th of August every year as Chopstick Day.

Japanese chopsticks are shorter than Chinese chopsticks. This is because in Japanese meals, each person has his own set of dishes. However, Chinese share the dishes at the same table, and therefore need longer chopsticks to pick up the food.

In Mongolia, chopsticks are used as dancing instruments in the once famous Chopstick Dance. In the dance, Mongolian ladies hold a bundle of red chopsticks in each hand, and used them to hit against their shoulders, waists, legs, feet, the ground, or the other bundle. The rhythms created are crisp, clear, strong and lively.

Communal chopsticks

Emperor Gao Zhong of the Tang Dynasty always used two sets of chopsticks and spoons when he dined; one set for taking dishes from the plates, and the other for eating. This is because he was normally served more dishes than he could eat, with the leftovers given to the maids and eunuchs. Emperor Gao Zhong, therefore, used two sets of cutlery to preserve the cleanliness of the food, and pioneered the use of communal chopsticks for common use.

The Significance of Chopsticks

Chopsticks and Social Status

143

Chopsticks and Sacrificial Offerings

Chopsticks and Marriage

Customs on the Use of Chopsticks

Chopstick Riddles and Chopstick Proverbs

Chopstick riddles
Two sisters of the same height, moving in and
out of the kitchen together. Sweet, sour, bitter,
or hot, they are always the first to taste. Two
brothers of the same height, they eat fish and
meat but they never grow any fat.

Chopstick proverbs
You can break a single chopstick, but not a bundle (unity is strength).

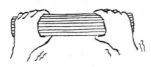

Two-part allegorical sayings. Build a
bridge with slender chopsticks — *nan
guo* (literally means 'hard to pass', but
actually means 'feeling miserable').

Hit the bell with a chopstick —
not a sound is heard.

147

Chopstick songs

Two little chopsticks make a good pair; one was lost in the Yangtze River. The lonely chopstick, longing for its missing lover to return. — *Yearning*, a Yunnan love song.

Brothers, please listen to me. Brothers, please listen to me. Brothers are like a pair of chopsticks, brothers are like a pair of bamboo strings.
— *Longing for dear ones* of the Lisu tribe.

We have to part even though we don't wish to; you have to leave me even though you don't want to. The pain is cutting open my heart; the pain is tearing out my liver. I send you off with tears in my eyes; I marry you off with tears running down my cheeks. We are like a pair of chopsticks torn apart; we are like a pair of small chicks separated.
— *Mother sending off the bride* of the Lisu tribe.

The secret codes of chopsticks and chopstick kung fu

What are you doing?

These two arrangements look like *zao* and *he* in Mandarin.

I'm copying the chopstick codes used by some early secret societies.

Zao is a signal calling for help.

There is also chopstick kung fu, which is an advanced form of Chinese martial arts.

The strength from the whole body is concentrated at the fingers and wrists, and exerted through the chopsticks.

He is the reply.

Chopsticks can also be used for self-defence or as a secret weapon to surprise the enemy.

Expressing Meanings with Chopsticks

Song Jing was the Prime Minister during the rule of Emperor Xuan Zong in the Tang Dynasty. He was an able man who was well loved by the court as well as the people.

One day, the emperor threw a banquet for his officials.

Minister Song, this pair of gold chopsticks suits you best.

Your Majesty, I don't understand.

This means your character is as straight as a pair of chopsticks.

Thank you, Your Majesty!

The don'ts of cooking

Food	Food that should not be consumed together
Chicken	Glutinous rice, plum, prawn. The heads of aged chickens are toxic and should be avoided.
Chicken egg	Persimmon. Balut (half-hatched duck egg) has germs and should be avoided.
Duck meat	Tree fungi, walnut
Pork meat	Prawn, crucian carp, soya bean, croton seed
Pork liver	Soya bean, bean curd, fish
Pork brain	Alcohol, salt. Should be avoided by those with high blood pressure, coronary heart disease, nephritis, arteriosclerosis.
Beef	Honey, corn, chestnut. Avoid cooking it together with fish.
Milk	Chocolate, egg, calcium powder
Mutton	Pumpkin, soya milk, cheese, preserved vegetables
Prawn	Chicken, pork, sugar, Vitamin C
Eel	Green eels are poisonous; yellow ones are safe.
Crab	Food with tannin
Cucumber	Avoid cooking it together with vegetables with high Vitamin C content.
Bamboo shoot	Bean curd, sugar
Radish	Persimmon, ginseng, knotweed tuber
Carrot	Radish, chilli, guava, papaya, tomato. Best served on its own or with meat.
Chinese chive	Spinach
Eggplant	Cuttlefish, crab. Avoid overripe eggplants as they are poisonous.
Bean curd	Milk, egg. Do not cook it together with spinach
Soya milk	Milk, egg. Do not cook it together with spinach
Apple, papaya	Seafood
Guava, grape	Seafood
Tangerine	Radish, milk
Mango	Garlic
Red bean	Do not cook it together with rice. Should be avoided by those with diuresis.
Onion	Honey, red date, red bayberry
Garlic	Tonic
Honey	Onion, garlic, Chinese chive
Alcohol	Coffee, soft drinks
Tea	Do not serve it with tonics.

Food to consume and avoid for common ailments

Ailment	Food to take	Food to avoid
Influenza	Watery gruel, rice water, noodle, fresh vegetables, fruits, soya milk, milk, fruit juices	Fried food, chilli, sweet or sour food
Cough	Vegetables, fruits, radish, loquat, honey, Job's tears	Hot and oily food, alcohol, seafood
Constipation	Vegetables, fruits, vegetable soups, soya milk, fruit juices, honey, sesame oil, soya bean, green bean	Hot and spicy food, alcohol, coffee, black tea
Insomnia	Vegetables, chicken, lean meat, lotus seed soup, lily soup	Oily and fried food
Headache	Fruits, chicken, pig liver, egg	Hot and spicy food, crab, prawn
Asthma	Radish, towel gourd, pear, tangerine, loquat, honey, fig, white gourd, black sesame, water melon, red date, carp	Alcohol, crab, prawn, chilli, soft drinks, soya bean, mustard leaf, pumpkin, fat meat, egg, sweet, salty or cold food
Diabetes	Soya bean, black soya bean, lean meat, fish, Chinese cabbage, white gourd, pumpkin, bitter gourd, radish, egg	Sugar, sugar cane, fruits, sweet potato, yam
High blood pressure	Celery, spinach, banana, haw, bamboo shoots, honey, green bean, kelp	Alcohol, black tea, coffee, chilli, innards, ovary and digestive glands of crabs, egg yolk
Chicken pox	Fresh vegetables	Seafood, hot and spicy food
Athlete's foot	Oat, millet, groundnut, broad bean, pig kidney, carp, onion, garlic, pepper, Job's tears soup	Raw and cold fruits, oily or salty food, seafood

Inedible food

- Meat that is dark brown or purple in colour; or that has red spots and no elasticity.
- Animal organs that have turned green.
- Decayed meat.
- Rotten chicken or duck eggs.
- Pork with grain-sized white spots.
- Fish with no internal organs.

- Crabs and prawns with unusual shapes.
- Food that has been touched by flies.
- Raw fruits.
- Rice that has been kept a long time.
- Tangerines that have turned bitter.
- Potatoes that have germinated.
- Yam with black spots.
- Vegetables that have turned yellow.

中华吃的故事

绘画 ：傅春江
翻译 ：丘耀鸿

 亚太图书有限公司出版